The Grace of God for You

Al Wilson

WESTBOW
P R E S S
A DIVISION OF THOMAS NELSON

WestBow Press books may be ordered through booksellers or by contacting:

WestBow Press
A Division of Thomas Nelson
1663 Liberty Drive
Bloomington, IN 47403
www.westbowpress.com
1-(866) 928-1240

ISBN: 978-1-4497-3596-8 (sc)

Library of Congress Control Number: 2011963678

Printed in the United States of America

WestBow Press rev. date:12/28/2011

Chapter 1

The grace of God is a living thing. It lives in God, and it is a strong force that constantly compels Him to love His children. He is constantly looking for way in which He can bless you. His love for you is far beyond anything you can understand.

If Jesus, the Son, would willingly die for you to save your soul from hell, and God, the Father, would willingly let His Son die such a horrible death on the cross for you, then why wouldn't He do anything else He could to help you?

If He died for you, why wouldn't He heal you? If He was willing to take all the beatings and torture in your place, for your sins, why wouldn't He do everything else He could to meet all of your other needs?

The Good News is, He has! He has already provided everything you will ever need. It was provided for you before you were ever born.

If you were expecting a new baby, wouldn't you prepare for it's arrival? Fix up his room, buy a baby crib, fill the room with toys, and everything else the child could possibly want.

Don't you think God the Father, who is Love, would do the same thing? You are His child. He loves you far more than you could ever possibly love your own child.

He is the perfect Father. His love is far above anything we could ever comprehend. He let His own Son suffer for your sake, just so He could adopt you into His family.

When you accepted Jesus as your Lord and Savior, Jesus took all of your sins, and gave you all of His righteousness. Jesus never committed any sin; you never committed any righteousness. But now, you have His righteousness. Now, when God the Father looks at you, He sees the righteousness of Jesus. He does not see your sin, not even a single little speck. He sees Jesus in you.

God the Father is holy. He cannot look on sin. Sin cannot exist in His presence. If He looked at you in your sin, you would instantly perish. But now, when He looks at you through the shed blood of Jesus, He sees righteousness; He sees you without sin.

Now you can come into His presence without fear. Now you can sit on your Father's knee, and feel His arms around you, and receive the love He has for you. Now you can experience the absolute fullness of joy that comes only in His presence.

Just imagine the heartache of a mother who had a baby daughter, but was unable to touch her, because if she did touch her she would instantly die. Imagine God the Father who longs to be with His children, who aches to hold them in His arms and tell them He loves them. But He can't, because if He touched them, they would die in His holy presence.

Because of His great love for you, He was willing to let His only son Jesus suffer and die in your place, so that now you can live in His presence.

God the Father ached and cried the day He watched his Son being beaten and tortured and finally dying on the cross. At the same time He looked forward to the joy of knowing that now His children could live in His presence. The daughter and son that before He couldn't touch, He can now hold in His arms. They can now laugh and play in His presence. They can hug and kiss their Father without fear.

Chapter 2

⌒

The grace of God is a free gift. Just receive it as a gift. There's nothing you have to do , or can do, to earn it. All of the gifts of God are freely given, but they are not meant for you alone. They are freely given to you, now you give them freely to others. Give to those who are in need, but especially give to those in the family of God.

God loves you. He loves to bless you, but He always uses others to bless you. When he blesses you financially, it is always through others. "Give, and it shall be given to you; a good measure, pressed down and shaken togethe3r (to make room for more), shall MEN give unto you." Money, silver and gold, are in the earth, not heaven. God has numerous ways to get the blessings to you, but it always comes through people.

By the grace of God, you are saved. Not by anything that you can do. All you have to do is just accept Jesus as you Lord and Savior, and God does all the rest. God always takes care of His children. Once you become a member of the royal family of God, your heavenly father will take care of you.

God is the perfect example of a loving, caring, father. He loves you beyond what you can even comprehend. His love is a sacrificial love. He let His own Son die, just so He could receive you into His family.

And if He loves so much that He would let His Son Jesus die for you, why wouldn't He freely, lavishly, bestow these other gifts to you? Why wouldn't He heal you? Why wouldn't He provide all the resources you would ever need? He would, He has, and He is. Even before the foundation of the world, He provided all the provisions you would ever need or want.

We are now approaching the End-times. The One World order is coming into power. The world as we knew it is constantly changing. Morallity is steadily declining. The United States of America is steadily declining. Violence, robberies, rapes, murders, and riots are on the increase. The current government regeime is anti-American, and completely out of control.

Sin is abounding everywhere. But always remember, where sin abounds, grace abounds much more. Hard times are coming, but God always takes care of His children. Those who belong to the kingdom of God don't need to worry. Stay under the shadow of His wing, and God will protect you. When every thing around you is sinking, just stand on the Rock.

It doesn't matter if America is going through inflation, depression, bankruptcy, or any other disaster, God's economy is still going strong. He still has streets of gold. Don't bother to watch the news media, keep the negative reports out of your mind. Keep the fear and the doubt out of your mind. Just keep your eye on Jesus, and follow Him. Listen to His instructions – and He WILL guide you through whatever the devil tries to throw at you.

The grace of God is beyond comprehension. Anytime you ask God for grace, He always hears you, and He always answers you. Anybody that asks for grace gets God's attention.

God is Love. He is always full of grace. His mercies are new every morning. He made a quality decision that He was going to love you, no matter what. He forgave you of all your sins two thousand years ago on the cross. Your past sins, your present sins, and your future sins, have ALL been forgiven.

All of your needs have already been provided for. Everything you will ever need in life has been provided for you, and layed up for you in heaven. You have a store house in heaven, just for you. It contains whatever you need or want. It contains healing, new body parts for those who are maimed, various anointing, various gifts of the Spirit, the power and the abilities to get wealth or obtain increase, and anything else that you might need.

Once you accepted Jesus, you became a member of the Royal family of God. You are an heir of all the things in heaven. You are co-heir with Jesus. Whatever Jesus has, you have. As a member of the kingdom of God you have the legal right to all that Jesus has.

God is not trying to hold anything back from you. He's trying to get things to you. Anything and everything you will ever need is already provided. It's already there, in the invisable realm, just waiting for you. You only have to reach out your hand of faith and possess it.

Chapter 3

⁓

Grace is a marvelous act of love from a Father to His children. Like love, grace is a decision our Father in heaven made to bestow upon us. It is not given because of anything we have done. It is an act of His great love. We didn't earn it. We can't buy it.

When you hold a little baby in your hands, you tenderly love it, and you take care of all its needs. You play with it, and you provide all it wants. The baby doesn't have to ask you for anything. You are there, 24/7, to give it whatever it might want. At the slightest sound that baby makes, you rush to help it, to let it know that you are there, to reassure it that there is nothing to be afraid of, or anything to worry about, because you are always there to meet all of its needs.

Multiply that love for your child by about 100 times, and you can begin to imagine how much your Father in heaven loves you. You are His child. He picked you out form all the people in the world, and chose you as His own.

He has lavishly bestowed all that He has upon you. All the blessings of Abraham are yours. All of your needs are met according to His glorious riches in Christ Jesus. He has provided healing for you. He said in Mark chapter 11 that whatever you want, need or desire He will give it to you. The Father loves you. The Holy Spirit has given you the power and ability to accomplish anything that you need to do. And Jesus has provided the wisdom of God to show you how. Jesus shed His own blood for you to save you; not only from hell, but also from anything else that you might need saving from. He has saved you from hell, from all the snares and traps of the devil, from all sickness and diseases, and from poverty and lack.

All that you have, or will ever need, has already been provided for you by His marvelous grace. It's been given in love; just receive it in love. You don't have to do anything; just receive it. That's what makes the love and the grace of God so wonderful. It's free! Just take it and unwrap it like you would a Christmas present, and enjoy it.

Jesus came that you might have life, and have it more abundantly. Life to the fullest, until it overflows, that your joy may be full and complete, lacking nothing, wanting nothing.

What amazing grace, that my God should die for me!

The grace of God is so pure and holly that most Christians can't accept it. They try to earn it, and when they can't, they give up. The grace, and the favor of God is not something you have to work for. All you have to do is just receive it. When you are given a gift, you just receive it.

God gives grace freely and without cost to whoever asks and ANYBODY that asks for grace, God never turns down! You're His child. He loves you. Why would He turn you down? Why would He let His Son die for you, and then NOT freely give you all things?

The Father is not trying to keep things from you. He's trying to get them to you. If your son wanted some bread, would you give him a stone? If your daughter wanted a new dress, would you her a snake? No, you would give them whatever they need. Even more so your Father in heaven will freely give you all things that you desire. He said that He would give you all the desires and all the secret petitions of your heart. Things that are just between you and the Father, that no one else knows about.

Even things that you have never told your spouse or your best friend. Things that nobody could ever know about except your Father. And He said He would give them to you.

Have you asked? If you don't ask you won't receive. But God said in Mk 11:23, 26 that whatever you ask in Jesus' name, and believe in your heart that you will have them, you will have whatsoever you ask.

Chapter 4

~

The grace of God is foremost given to those whom God choses. It is not available to everybody. Grace is something you have to ask for – but it IS available to anybody who asks. Grace is not only given to you freely, it is available to help you obtain whatever you need.

Grace is a substance. It is manifested into reality whenever you ask for it. God will never turn you down when you ask for grace.

Grace is free. Grace is love. It is a free gift to anyone who asks for it.

Jesus, before the cross, asked for grace to endure. And because that grace was flowing in Him, He forgave the thief that was on the cross next to Him.

God is love. God is full of grace. God is long-suffering. Because of His grace and love for you, He will wait, sometimes for years, for you to come to Him, and ask for forgiveness and salvation. Anytime, anywhere, that anyone asks for forgiveness, He is always ready and willing to forgive them and save them. The Bible says He is quick to forgive anybody that asks. The very second you repent-you are forgiven.

Also, the very second that you are forgiven, God puts it (your sin) out of His memory. All of your sins have been forgiven-and forgotten. He can do that, He's God. So don't ever remind God of some past sin; He's forgotten about it. And if He has forgotten about it, so should you. You are a new creation in Christ. The past is dead. After Abraham had repented, God treated him as if he had never sinned. He will do the same for you. Every day is a new beginning.

A lot of times we think we have missed God. Maybe because of something we've done that was out of the will of God. Or maybe something that we didn't do that we should have. Or maybe because of some sin, or disobedience. We think we have missed our calling that God put on our lives, and that we are totally out of His will. We messed up so bad that when we do repent and come back to God, we think God will have to switch over to plan "B", or plan "C", or "D". This is not how God looks at our lives. In God's mind, there is no plan "B". Whenever we come back to God, He immediately puts us back in the center of plan "A". We can pick up right where we left off years ago. So, even if you feel like you missed God, don't run from Him. Run to Him. Get back in plan "Λ". God loves you. He wants what is best for you. Your sins are forgiven—and forgotten. You can now start over in the perfect will of God. Praise God!

It is very important to realize, now that God has erased all of your past sins from His memory, that His mind is now a blank page. What do you want God to remember about you? What do you want to write on the blank page of His memory? (Hint!). I am blessed! I am healed! I am Prosperous! I am ------------------------! "My grace is sufficient, for all your needs, whatever they are. The problem is, do you really believe that I can work a miracle for YOU? You believe I can work a miracle for Kenneth Hagin, but do you really believe I can perform a miracle in your situation? It's easy to believe that Joe Christian can receive miracles. He's strong in faith, but how about you? I said in My word that when you accept Jesus as your Lord and Savior, you instantly became a member of the family of God, and heir to all the promises. All the blessings of Abraham are now yours." Love, the Father.

Chapter 5

~

God loves His children. The value of anything is determined by how much someone is willing to pay for it. A gold coin could be worth $100, or $2,000, depending on the buyer. God loves you so much that He let His only Son die in your place. Jesus loves you so much that He was willing to suffer and die on the cross so He could save you from going to hell, and that you could live with Him forever in heaven. God gives everybody a choice. He is a Gentleman; He will not force you to follow Jesus. You can choose death, or you can choose life. You can choose sickness, or your can choose health. You can choose the devil, or you can choose Jesus. (If you do not choose Jesus, then by default you have chosen the devil, and all of the punishments and tortures that go with him, and you will be separated from God for all eternity). Hint: choose God! Choose life! But you have to make that decision. It's your chose.

Why would God love me so much? He created the earth, stars, planets, and all of the universe. Why should He care about me, or even know that I exist? God doesn't just love, He IS love. He made a decision, a commitment to love you even before you were born. The stars, planets, and things are marvelous creations, but things don't love. God made us in His image. We want to love, and to be loved. God wants to love, to give. That's why He made us. His desire to have children was so great that He created the human race. And, like any parent, He would die to protect His children. When we started to go astray, like lost sheep, He sent Jesus to get us back on track, to show us the way home, back to the Father.

God wants us to accept Him, to love Him, but He is not going to force you. We are not puppets, He gave us a free will. We have a choice. We can choose to follow Jesus, and if we don't, then by default we choose to follow the devil. But it is our choice.

God loves you, but He will let you go to hell, if that's your choice. That's not His will, but He won't force you to love Him.

When you do choose Jesus, you immediately become co-heirs with Him, and receive all the wonderful benefits that heaven provides. By His marvelous grace God choose to love you just as much as He loves Jesus. As a co-heir, you have access to all that Jesus has.

But remember, Jesus is the way, the truth, and the light. He is the ONLY way to heaven. Without Him, you are lost, and doomed to spend eternity in hell.

Your spirit man will live forever, somewhere. Where you spend eternity is entirely up to you.

Jesus came that you might be set free, and if you accept Jesus you are free indeed. Anything that tries to bind you, restrict you, or put limitations on you, is from the devil. It is not from God.

When you accepted Jesus, you received all of His blessings, and by the grace of God He has removed all limitations from you. Do not allow Satan to put any boundaries on your life again.

You are God's child Imitate your Father. That's what your big brother Jesus did. He said, "I only do what I see My Father do." All children imitate their parents. We should do the same thing with our heavenly Father. You can't go wrong by doing what God does.

Speak to your mountain of debt. Jesus did. Speak to sicknesses and diseases. Tell them to depart. Jesus did. Speak to whatever problem you have, and watch it leave. Jesus did. Act just like your big brother. Get the same results Jesus got. The same Holy Spirit that was in Jesus is now in you. Your words have the same power as they did when Jesus spoke them.

"My grace is sufficient to meet all your needs. Whatever you want, whatever you need, My Grace will supply. Everything you need, everything you want has already been provided."

God made provisions for your every need even before the foundation of the world. As a child of

God, all you have to do is just claim it. God has given you the kingdom, and all the fullness therein.

Most Christians are not walking in the fullness of God, either because they think these blessings are just too good to be true, or they just don't know; they suffer because of a lack of knowledge.

It's very important to spend time studying the word of God. Find out who you are in Christ.

It's very important to spend time with your Father. Get in His presence. Talk to Him. Listen to Him. All of your burdens are lifted when you get in His presence. And stay there. The more time you spend in His presence, the more answers you will receive to your problems.

The more you die to yourself, the more you receive from Him.

Chapter 6

If you want to activate the blessings of God, you have to do something. God has given you His Word. He cannot lie. If you speak to the mountain, God will make sure that it moves. He said it. He has already provided everything we will ever need, but we have to use our faith to get it.

Salvation has already been provided—for everybody on earth—but we are not going to be saved until we ask for it.

Healing has already been provided—by His stripes we HAVE BEEN healed—but we are not going to be healed until we stand on His Word and claim it.

All of the promises of God are conditional. God has made them available to us, but we have to receive them.

"I love My children. I want to be with them. All you have to do is call Me closer. I will come. Withdraw from the world, and come within, to the Holy of Holies in your heart. That's where I live. I am always here. I yearn to be with you, to fill you with My peace, My joy.

No earthy Father desires to do more for his children than I do, if you would just let Me."

"To have a close relationship with Me, everything in you must die. Humble yourself before Me. Spend time in My presence. Then I will show you how My Word meets all of your needs, and My promises will be a source of rest to you.

I always keep My Word. I always keep My covenants. If you believe, then you can rest in Me, knowing that I have already provided, before the foundation of the world, everything you will ever need."

"I am the Lord your God. I have made you, and I will take care of you. Didn't I tell you in My Word that I would love you forever? I loved you before you were born. I have already provided everything you will ever need, even before you were born.

"I never change. I love you today, and I will love you tomorrow. I love you with an everlasting love. That love will not cease, no matter what you do.

I am your Father, and you are always welcome in My presence."

Lord, but by your grace we would have all ended up in hell.

By the grace of the Father, He left His dear Son suffer and die on the cross for us. By the grace of the Son, He was willing to take our place and suffer the agonizing pain, the humiliation, taking every disease in the world into His body, going into the depths of hell and suffered even more beatings at the hands of the demons, laughed at by Satan; all of this so we wouldn't have to, just so we could go to heaven and be with him.

What amazing grace, that God should die for me. Even if I had been the only person on earth, Jesus would have died for me.

Have you ever thought of yourself as being so wonderful that someone would be willing to die for you? Jesus does. Your heavenly Father does. Jesus Himself said that your Father loves you just as much as He loves Jesus.

The grace of God is what faith in God is based on. His children come to Him because of His great love, not because of His power. Throughout the Holy Bible, the prophets talk about the love and the abundant grace of God, never about His ability, strength, or his power.

Why? Because love is greater than all these things. Love is the greatest power in all the universe. Power or might can never conquer the heart – but love does. The love of a child can conquer the heart of the strongest man on earth.

Love can rule the nations. The kingdom of God is ruled by love. Citizens obey the king because of their love for Him, not out of fear.

Satan tries to control his subjects by fear. And he is losing thousands of people daily. Once people realize just how much God loves them, and that He is ready, willing, and able to save them from their sins, afflictions, additions, diseases, and whatever else problem they might have, they gladly accept Jesus as their Lord. They run to Him with open arms, and away from Satan. And as hard as Satan tries, he can't stop them.

Once you have decided to accept Jesus there's not a thing he can do to stop you. If he could stop you, believe me, he would, but he can't.

Chapter 7

One of the keys to understanding the truths of the Bible is having a revelation of the gift of grace. The way we enter into grace is through faith.

Grace is unmerited favor, but even more than that, it is God's willingness to use His power and His ability on our behalf, even though we don't deserve it. The only way we can have peace with God, and access into His grace (willingness) is through faith in His Word and the blood of Jesus His Son.

We cannot merit favor with God through good works. It is by faith that we might enter into the promises through grace. Under the New Covenant, it is through mercy and grace that we are justified by faith, not by what we have done, but by faith in the blood of Jesus. It is through faith that we access the grace of God for the remission of our sins.

Most people believe God is able, but they are not sure if He is willing. We need a revelation of the gift of grace, and just receive God's willingness to pour out His blessings upon us.

The more you know about what God will do, the more willing He is to do it, because that knowledge produces faith. God is already willing, but His willingness is multiplicd when you know what God will do on your behalf.

By grace you are saved through faith; not of yourself, it (grace) is the gift of God. Grace is given to every one of us according to the measure of the gift of Christ.

The death of Jesus ushered in the dispensation of grace. The Word (Jesus) was made flesh, and dwelt among us, and we beheld His glory, and He was full of grace and truth. He was filled with the same willingness to bless us as was the Father.

The Word of God is the Word of grace. In the beginning was the Word, and the Word was with God, and the Word was God. The Bible is the Word of God's willingness toward us.

You know the grace of our Lord Jesus Christ, that, though He was rich, He willingly became poor for your sake, that you might be rich. That includes financially, spiritually, physically, and every way.

Be strong in grace. Know that God is able. Know that God is willing.

Grow in grace. Don't stay where you are. As you grow in the grace of God, you will realize that your Father wants you to have the things He has provided for you. He has given us all things that pertain to life and godliness. He has given exceeding great and precious promises, that we might be part of His divine nature, and escape the corruption that is in the world.

And God cannot lie. He ALWAYS keeps His promises!

Without faith, it is impossible to please Him. When you come to God, you must believe that He really exists, and that He will reward those who diligently seek Him.

God is not pleased when you don't have enough faith to enter into the grace that He has already given you through the precious promises.

So come boldly to the throne of grace, not begging, that you may obtain mercy, and find grace to help you in your time of need.

Where sin abounds, grace superabounds. Grace swallowed ALL our sins. Sin used to control us, but now grace reigns through righteousness unto eternal life by Jesus Christ our Lord. We receive an abundance of grace, and the gift of righteousness, and we reign in life in Christ Jesus.

You can allow sin to control you, or you can allow grace (God's willingness) to reign in your life. The choice is yours and time is short. Enter into His grace through faith and trust God and His promises today.

Boldly declare; "I am free! I am debt free! Sickness free! I am free from the curse! I serve my God with joyfulness and gladness. Jesus, I sit with You on the throne of grace. I am above – I will never be beneath. I am the head—I will never be the tail. I am strong. I am established in the blessing. I am the seed of Abraham. I receive hope and great peace. For this I am eternally grateful."

In 2 Cor 12:8 when Paul was being harassed by a demon, he asked Jesus to remove it.

God responded, "My grace, My favor and loving kindness is sufficient for your every need. My enabling grace, the goodness of God which is carried out by the Holy Spirit is enough to enable you to overcome any trouble or danger. My strength is made perfect, fulfilled and complete in your weakness."

We as believers are weak, and sometimes the Lord makes us even weaker, so that we then depend solely upon Him, thereby obtaining His strength. The strength of Christ can be exhibited through me, but only when I know I am weak, only when I know I can do nothing without Him.

Jesus didn't tell Paul "No." He simply said, "Paul, My power is already available to you, but you have to activate it. You speak to the mountain, the devil, or whatever is hindering you. You command it to go. It will obey you. I have given you authority over all devils and demons, over all sickness and diseases, over finances, and over everything that flies, swims, or creeps on the earth, so that nothing should be able to hurt you or hinder you."

Paul then answered, "I will gladly glory in my weakness and infirmaties, that the strength and power of Christ the Anointed One may rest and dwell in me. For when I am weak in my human strength, then I am truly strong and powerful in divine strength."

Chapter 8

~

"The grace of God is always present, everywhere. Everytime My children ask for grace, I always answer them. My grace is always available, to anyone who asks."

You may say, "I have sinned, strayed from God and gone my own way. How can God use me now?"

"I have never left you. I have never left you without hope. I have always been there with you, ready to forgive, ready to start over. You are My child. All have made mistake and fallen short, but I have never abandoned you."

"Do not try to do things your way, with your own understanding. Listen to the Holy Spirit, let Him guide you in the way you should go. Together we will accomplish what I have called you to do.

Trust in God. Honor Me, and I will honor you. I have already provided everything you will ever need to fulfill your calling. I called you. I choose you. So, now you will have to be successful.

I have given you skills and talents, but none of them will work without the Holy Spirit, without the grace of God on you. Listen, with all your heart, and mind, and I will guide you in the way you should go."

"Do you feel alone? Forgotten? My grace is sufficient. Have you reached the end of the line, the end of your rope? My grace is sufficient.

Draw near to Me, and I will draw near to you. In My presence you will find rest, peace, joy. In My presence all of your questions will be answered, and all of your needs will be met. But only in My presence will you receive the blessings. Knock, and the door will be open to you, but you have to knock. Ask, and you will receive, but you have to ask."

"I am your Father, and no earthly father wants to do more for his children than I do. If you will ask, in faith, believing, I will give you the desires of your heart.

First you must die to yourself. Everything in you must die. Then you will call on Me, and I will answer. Then you can speak to your mountain, and it will depart. But only in My presence."

The Name of God is LOVE. He has always been Love, and He always will be Love. He IS LOVE. When ever you think of your heavenly Father, think of Him as Love. The Father, who is Love, wants to be with His children, as any earthly father or mother would.

Spend some time in the presence of your Father. Experience what real love is. True unconditional love. He wants to be with you, more than you can imagine. Not to receive anything from you, but just to give. The heart of any real father is to give to his children. Even more so with your heavenly Father. He created his children just to have somebody to love, someone to spend time with, someone to pal around with.

He created you to be His friend, His buddy. He wants you to go fishing with Him, to watch the ball game together, to spend the day shopping together.

Come into his presence, not to receive, but just to tell Him you love Him, and experience the depths of that unconditional, everlasting, deep, deep love.

The love of God and the grace of God is a never-ending source of joy for God's people. You can live in that place of peace and contendment, no matter what may be going on around you.

Come to Jesus now, and receive that peace. Let Him fill you with that ever-lasting joy. No matter what the world is going through, you can still have that inner peace, just knowing that your heavenly Father is always with you, He will never forsake you, and He will never fail you. He will ALWAYS be there when you need Him. The love of God is always present everywhere.

Chapter 9

Mat 8:13 God has made abundant provisions for us through the promises in the New Testament.

Rom 5:17 We receive an abundance of grace and the gift of righteousness and will reign as kings in life by Christ Jesus.

Grace is God's willingness to use His power and His ability on your behalf even though you don't deserve it. God has made provisions for us, but to receive what He has given, we must believe it, and then mix faith with God's words. Unless we take hold of the truth of God's word and mix faith with it, we will never receive the manifestation of these promises, even though it is God's will for us to do so.

"I have never left you. I have never forsaken you. You are My child. I want you to have an abundant life. I want you to live in all the fullness of God. But – it's your choice. I told the children of Israel to choose life or death, health or sickness, riches or poverty, Jesus or the devil. It's your decision. I can't make it for you. I will not force people to choose Me, or to love Me. It's got to be from a willing heart. True love is given, it cannot be taken. I made a decision to love you. I give you the same choice."

We are in a race. A race of time to that last minute when Jesus comes. The rapture is going to occur, and occur very soon. We need God's grace to complete our calling, our purpose for being here, before the rapture occurs.

The main goal for the child of God right now is to save souls, to help prevent those who are lost from going to hell. This might be their last chance. You might be their last chance. There is an urgency in these last days, these last few hours of time, to reach those who are lost with the Gospel of Christ, to teach them of the love of Christ Jesus, and to let them know that they don't have to perish in hell with the devil, but that they can live in heaven forever with Jesus who died to save them.

Chapter 10

~

Jesus as the Son of God came to earth in the flesh, redeeming man by becoming our substitutionary sacrifice, and then defeating death in resurrection life and making that life available to all who believe.

We open ourselves to this resurrection life and the power of God through grace. Grace is an important, yet often overlooked, element in our faith.

Grace is used throughout the Bible synonymously with the anointing or power of God.

The grace of God opens the door to heaven as well as to a quality of life on this earth that is not overwise attainable.

Eph 2:4 God is so rich in His mercy! In order to satisfy the great, wonderful and intense love He has for us, that even when we were spiritually dead, slain by our own shortcomings and Trespasses, he made us alive together in fellowship and in union with Christ. He gave us the very life of Christ Himself, the same new life with which He reserected Jesus, for it is by grace, God's favor and mercy which you did not deserve, that you are saved, delivered from judgement, and made partakers of Christ's salvation.

God raised us up together with Christ and gave us joint seats with Him in the heavenly spere by virtue of our being in Christ Jesus.

He did this that He might clearly demonstrate through the ages to come the exceeding, immeasurable, and limitless riches of His free grace in His kindness and goodness of heart toward us through Christ Jesus. For it is by His free grace that you are saved and delivered from judgement and made partakers of Christ's salvation through your faith. This salvation is not of yourselves. It did not come through your own striving; it is the gift of God. It is not the result of what anyone can possibly do, so no one can boast in himself or take glory to himself.

We are saved by grace through faith. We can't do enough good works to earn our way into heaven or experience the benefit of salvation. We can't do anything to earn salvation. That's why it's called grace.

When we hear the word "saved," ninety-nine percent of us think of going to heaven, but the Greek word "sozo" means a lot more than that. It also means: "preservation, provision, protection, deliverance." It's translated as "healing" on several occasions in the New Testament. This is a word that touches every aspect of human life.

Jesus shed His blood to save you, and that blood has saved you from every thing you need to be saved from.

This salvation is something that comes to us only by the grace of God. If we don't understand the grace of God and its operation in our lives, then we will limit the things that salvation will do for us. Whether it's healing, protection, or deliverance, you need an understanding not only of what the grace of God is defined as but its application to our lifestyles in order to experience its fullness.

God's grace is sufficient to deliver us from anything the enemy is doing. When you understand your inability to deal successfully with life's challenges on your own and humble yourself before god, He can then bring His grace – the power of Christ – upon you to produce the deliverance you desire.

1 Pet 5;5 You who are younger, be subject to the ministers and spiritual guides of the church, giving them due respect and yielding to their counsel. All of you clothe yourselves with humility. God sets Himself against the proud, the insolent, and the boastful, but He gives grace, favor, and blessings to those who are humble.

Therefore, humble yourselves under the mighty hand of God, that He may exalt you in due time, casting all of your cares, worries, and anxieties upon him, for He cares for you and loves you.

God doesn't do bad things to humble you. However, if you're going your own way, it will eventually bring you to your knees. You will be confronted with the fact that you're powerless to generate a meaningful life outside the grace of God.

The Lord doesn't want you to have to learn that way. He docsn't want you to bc humbled by your circumstances or the enemy of your soul. It's His will that you humble yourself.

When we humble ourselves, the grace and power of God are made available to us. These things only work within the environment of humility.

If we want to access the power and grace of God, it is extremely important for us to understand conceptually what humility is.

In a basic sence, humility is a refusal to exalt one's self. It is an acknowledgement of your inability without God to produce anything that will bring contentment in this life.

You cannot do anything to find fulfillment or contentment in this life outside the grace of God. That heart recognition is where humility begins.

Humility doesn't mean you let yourself get walked on by the circumstances of life and never raise a defense against what might come your way. Humility has to be interpreted within the context of other scriptures such as "I can do all things through Christ who strengthens me." (Phil 4:13) and "we are more than conquerors through Him that loves us."

Without God, you can do nothing; with God, you can do all things. Period. This is what genuine humility is – a heart recognition that without the Lord, you can't pull it off; but with God you can do all things. God gives grace to the people who have this recognition. And thank God we're never without Him! He never leaves us; He never forsakes us! The Spirit of victory is in us, and with Christ we always get the victory!

When you submit yourself to the Lord, God will exalt you in due time. His time. It is God's will to exalt you. As He works in you, a little time ma pass, but He's going to give you more and more visibility, more and more influence, more and more increase and success (that's what exalt is), because you're living for Him and your life will make the kind of statement that will glorify Him – not yourself.

James 4:6 He gives us more and more grace, and the power of the Holy Spirit to overcome all evil. God resists and sets Himself against the proud and haughty, but gives grace continually to those who are humble enough to receive it.

Be subject to God; submit yourself to Him. Resist the devil, stand firm against him, and he will flee from you.

Come close to God, and He will come close to you. Humble yourself in His presence, and He will exalt you, lift you up, and make your life significant.

This verse reiterates the fact that humility opens you to the grace of God. It also shows us that you can't successfully resist the devil until you're humbled yourself before God.

Humility is absolutely necessary. We have to understand the need for us to acknowledge from our hearts our inability without God. Because this is the environment within which grace operates.

Eph 2:8 says "It is by grace you are saved through faith." So it is through the operation of your faith that grace is appropriated.

Grace has to be the focus of our faith for any of the benefits of salvation to come our way.

Certainly, you do need to know and believe what God has promised you and what His covenant provisions for your life are, but once you have made grace your focus, then God can and will work to bring you all the benefits of salvation.

Isn't the grace of God wonderful?

CLOSING WORDS

As a king and a priest, I am a representative of the grace of God.

How does grace work?

1. Grace releases supernatural
   Strength to keep going, and ignites
   In us the determination to never
   Quit no matter what.

2. Grace echoes in our spirit,
   Constantly reminding us that God
   Is always with us to support us.

3. Grace keeps pointing us to God's
   Goal of teaching us and molding us
   Into His image.

4. Grace reminds us that our Father
    Enables us to become stronger in
    Faith and with deeper intimacy.

5. Grace ensures us that God is in
    Control. He has set limits on what
    The devil can do, and He has given
    Us authority over ALL the works
    Of the evil one.

6. Grace awakens our faith with
    Conviction that God can and will
    Turn our tough times into something
    Good, and we will have total
    Complete recovery.

7. Grace reminds us that God never
   Leaves us; He is a true friend that
   Sticks closer to us than a brother.

8. Grace reminds us that we have a
   Blood – bought right to live the
   Abundant life that Jesus provided.

Our abundance has been paid for by the precious blood of Jesus.

Everything I have is by the grace of God.

Postscript

~

WHERE DO I GO WHEN I DIE?

God, in His mercy, sent His Son Jesus to take the punishment for our sin. He died in our place, rose from the grave, and now lives in heaven. Everyone who believes and accepts Jesus as their lord will be saved and go to heaven after death. Those who don't believe will go to hell and spend eternity with the devil.

Where you go when you die depends on what you do with Jesus. God always gives us a choice. We can choose Jesus, or, if not, then be default we choose the devil. No one goes to heaven except through Jesus. You have to choose!

Say this simple prayer: "Jesus, I repent of my sins and confess that you are the only way of salvation for me. Help me in this life; and when I die, take me to heaven to be with You. Amen."